LOVE AND ARMOUR

Glenn Martin

G.P. Martin Publishing

Published by G.P. Martin Publishing
5 Gumnut Place
Cherrybrook NSW 2126
www.glennmartin.com.au

© Glenn Martin 2007
First published 2007. Reprinted 2017.

All rights reserved. No part of this publication may be reproduced, stored in a retrieval system, or transmitted in any form or by any means, electronic, mechanical, photocopying, recording or otherwise, without the prior written permission of the publisher.

National Library of Australia
Cataloguing-in-Publication Entry

Martin, Glenn.
    Love and armour.
    ISBN 978 0 6480811 1 1 (pbk)
    1. Martin, Glenn. I. Title.
    A828.409

Book layout and design by Glenn Martin
Typeset in Palatino Linotype 11 pt

The only thing we did that was wrong
was to stay in the wilderness
for too long.

Tony Newman; from a book of songs and inspiration by Tony Newman and Peter Stone: *Travelling to freedom*, LPS Publishing, Harbord, 1971.

Preface

This is my second collection of poems. The first was *Flames in the open*, a selection from between 1970 and 1988. The selection of poems here is another slice from the same period of time. I made this selection in 1989, and published it for just a few friends, inventing Bywater Whimsies as a publishing entity – a figment.

Bywater was "real". When I moved to my Horseshoe Creek house, 17 kilometres out from Kyogle on the far north coast of New South Wales, in January 1978, I named it Bywater. It was the name of the area near Hobbiton, where Bilbo Baggins lived in J.R.R. Tolkein's *The Hobbit* and *Lord of the Rings*.

In 1989 I was living alone. My partner had left the year before, in a downward spiral, going back to her parents in Sydney, and she had taken our son with her. He was five years old then.

I didn't put the poems in chronological order, and I like the sequence as I put it then. The poems cover my perceptions over a long period, the vicissitudes of relationships, feelings, and my striving for meaning. When I was younger (to be clearer, less than 25), I dated poems and kept the original piece of paper. Some of my friends think this is odd, but the poems were about particular moments in time, so I think there is some sense in my keeping the pieces of paper.

I wrote on scraps of waste paper that represented things that were part of my life at the time (e.g. worksheets I used in the classroom as a teacher). I learned recently that Kurt Vonnegut did the same – more boldly, he crafted (or assembled?) entire novels on stray scraps of paper. I don't feel so outlandish with him for company.

This is even more intriguing to me now, as I can place the poems in the context of what was happening at the time. In some cases, the context is still vivid, and in other cases the poem has assumed its own life and its roots have been cut (shall we say?) asunder.

As I said in *Flames in the open*, in my stories I am not trying to interpret or interfere with the poems, I'm just offering a context where I think it is illuminating. Growing up and reading Australian poets, I was annoyed and alienated when they quoted obscure references that I was most unlikely to know. I felt that poems should communicate and connect, not flaunt esotericism.

I haven't rewritten any of these poems. They are as I encapsulated them in 1989. Is this important? To me, yes. This collection is in some ways a retrospective. The earliest ones in particular reflect the crude influence of poets I had only recently discovered; or the volatile environment of the early 1970s.

This is very much why I still enjoy them now, in the same way that you would not want the Rolling Stones to issue a "mature" version of "Satisfaction" that cleaned up its juvenile rawness.

The opening quote: "The only thing we did that was wrong, was to stay in the wilderness for too long", is by Michael Newman, a Catholic priest who put together a great book of songs and stories in 1971 that summoned up so much of the turbulence and aspirations of that time (the year before it was Gough Whitlam's "time"). The book was a collection of Christian and social activist songs. The saying appealed to me and still does.

What does it mean? I take it to be a "prodigal son" concept – everybody comes home sooner or later. Jon Anderson (from Yes) captured that sentiment most perfectly in the song "Somehow I'll find my way home" on the *Friends of Mr Cairo* album (circa 1980). Ursula Le Guin addressed it more recently in a collection of stories called *Always Coming Home*.

I suppose Newman was championing the homely virtues of the Catholic Church. The irony was that around that time I was coming to the conclusion that the Anglican Church, or indeed, any church, was no home for me. But I've always remembered the saying, to keep me from being obstinately alone or aloof from others.

Images

The photo on the front cover is from the Woodford Folk Festival (Queensland), December 2004.

The photo on the back cover is also from the Woodford Folk Festival, December 2005. The photos were taken by me.

I love the three ladies on the front cover. I think of the New Testament – love, hope and charity. I think of the three muses. I think of numerology, and the Tao – how one becomes two, then three, then the ten thousand things. First there is one, then yin and yang, then the three muses. One festival which embraces all, and three muses. Love and armour – love and our defences against hurt.

The three ladies were standing on long steel poles which were anchored in pivot points on the ground. The poles were curved, and the ladies were strapped to them at the ankles as if to a pogo stick, and looking like crocheted toilet roll holders. They were not static; the poles were gyrating in time to music, so my catching them at just that moment was magic. It's my favourite photo.

At Woodford Folk Festival there were many night acts like this as you walked around. You simply came upon them, or they came upon you. On mid-summer nights among crowds of people who had come as if to a respite (six days of it), where hate, anger, delusion and domination were unnecessary and irrelevant.

So why wouldn't I choose that as my front-page image?

And on the back cover? Again, Woodford. If love and armour were to contend, they would make an image like this, where there is somewhat confusion, but the ambience is benign. The need for defence is but an illusion. In the morning, we know we will laugh at how we stumbled in the dark. Even the music would be angled towards wry humour, soft cadences, lilting. Darkness it would pick up and turn to playful taunting performance which will have its time.

The import of the dark is ritual gestures that denote the great balance. Between love and armour there is poise, and afterwards there is the stillness where all things are possible.

Contents

Preface 1
Images 4
Contents 6
ADVANCING IN EMPTINESS 9
THE BADLANDS 10
IMAGES OF PERFECTION 11
BENJAMIN WOODCUTTER AND THE QUEEN 12
WANTING 13
A DARK DAY THEN 14
PAINT ME A PICTURE 15
YELLOW SMOKE ON THE WATER 16
A DEAD MAN 18
FAR AWAY 19
THERE IS NONE THAT SEES TOO FAR 20
CYNICAL MOMENT 22
THE SOFT BARRAGE 23
RIVERRUNDOWN 24
COMRADES 26
FOND HEARTS 27
JOY AND SORROW 28
FOR A CITY FRIEND 30
BIRTH DAY 32
FOREST/NIGHT/HOUSE LAMPS 33
MING I 34
THE READING 35
IN DANGER 36
THE OLD MEN HAVE A SAYING 37
THE DRY WELL (Ching) 38

THE SAGE'S UNDERTAKINGS	39
THE SAGE AS STRANGER	40
KU'N (RECEPTIVE)	41
THE LAST SONG	42
THE LAST SUPPER	43
THE NOTEBOOK	44
Advancing in emptiness	44
The badlands	45
Images of perfection	45
Benjamin woodcutter and the queen	47
Wanting	48
A dark day then	49
Paint me a picture	52
Yellow smoke on the water	54
A dead man	55
Far away	61
There is none that sees too far	61
Cynical moment	63
The soft barrage	64
Riverrundown	65
Comrades	66
Fond hearts	71
Joy and sorrow	74
For a city friend	76
Birth day	81
Forest/night/house lamps	85
Ming I: Darkening of the light	85
The reading	89
In danger	89
The old men have a saying	94
The dry well (Ching)	95

The sage's undertakings 101
The sage as stranger 102
K'un (Receptive) 104
The last song 109
The last supper 109
The end 113
The author 114

ADVANCING IN EMPTINESS

He advances by enhancing what men see as inferior;
He reveres what men call emptiness.

This is why Jesus walked on water,
and as the Risen One
disappeared through walls.

Men say of a thing, it is lost,
but what is lost?
It is easily restored.

Such truths go on forever,
appearing, disappearing,
like the golden heart
of the sun through mist.

Like the chance ray of light,
the thread runs secure,
anchored from ship to shore.

THE BADLANDS

Gather up your heart and hurry on:
do you sense the badlands around you?
Now you need to wear armour
And keep alert.

There will be small safe zones
where musicians can tame the evils,
but you must not stay there too long
or your strength will be sapped.

You are sick,
You are weak, confused:
It is the badlands; it is not the end.

Gather your heart and move,
Seek out the return of joy.

The essential truth lives,
heart shall be released
at its destination,
the feast prepared,
child protected,
the secrets declared,
time connected, ever.

IMAGES OF PERFECTION

Half a mile from home —
being that close is a rare gift,
one more lift
before the magic release
when you can ease yourself back
into gentler days.
Hard as a bronze fist
are our ways —
I have learnt the necessities
and seen sleek images of perfection:
the flawless men and their mates,
smooth and powerful as gods.
In a smaller way
I make it, break it, fake it,
Living in candle-light
to keep out the dark.
You live or you lose,
stand guard on your fragility.

And my dreams I keep for dark nights:
when the spotlight shines I dance.
Only some stupid creatures stand transfixed,
kangaroos, and are shot down
in the briefest shower of blood.
No creature am I of rare gifts.

BENJAMIN WOODCUTTER AND THE QUEEN

Come into my parlour, said the Queen.
The roof is made of fortified glass.
You may see the stars
twinkling like the fuses on dynamite sticks.
> It's not half nice here.
> Will tea be served soon?
> Will the crockery be dainty? Will there be a silver spoon?

Get your head down, said the Queen.
The bullets come whistling through.
What I'm to do about the holes in the furniture
I just don't know. It's a strain.
> Is that the Wondrous Mountain I can see?
> Oh, I do appreciate it.
> My own humble house is quite hidden,
> But standing on the lounge I can locate it.

Here's your tea in a bucket, said the Queen.
We don't use the cups on Tuesdays.
Take it into the corner and sip it;
the sugar is next to the cyanide under the table.
> Oh, thank you, I must be going.
> It's been dreadfully nice all the same.
> You've been so sweet I just don't deserve it;
> Will you tell the cook's daughter I came?

WANTING

I want to be
two-legged walking,
two-armed swinging,
head high, grinning,
hair flowing.
I want to see
grass at my feet,
march a country mile
and not meet
a wall, and instead
of ceilings, sky above my head.
As graceful as autumn leaves,
loose as a flag,
I want to colour the earth.

A DARK DAY THEN

And you would say we were no higher than the grass,
and you would tell me that like flowers we would pass:
it was a dark day when I knew you,
I have set my sights for the sun,
as straight as the barrel of a gun.

And you would weigh heavily like sad news in the morning,
or you would turn in terror, and stun me without warning:
it was a dark day when I knew you,
the shadows bore your weight,
but I have withdrawn from the chaos of your fate.

And you would be quizzical like unexpected sunlight,
and you would be suddenly passionate, almost bright,
it was a dark day when I knew you,
I took your ecstatic moments then;
I stand alone, you've lost your way again.

PAINT ME A PICTURE

Paint me a picture
of someone's sedate afternoon,
as solid as you please,
to hang on the wall of my room.
We are changing;
you never impeach me in some sudden tirade:
you reproach me in silence,
and the words you do speak mount a barricade.
> We know what is different,
> enough to own when time is progress,
> but we are out here now alone,
> having to question what we possess.

Each moment that we take
we stand on a razor's edge,
and on one of these we fell separate:
have you withdrawn your pledge?
I'm holding on —
to the bare wires of what we had,
pressed into breaking silence —
has the dream gone bad?
> No longer are we children,
> but it's not worry about getting older;
> and I can make it without you,
> but a little harder, a little colder.

YELLOW SMOKE ON THE WATER

Yellow smoke on the water
from the round pot of moon
      in the sky —
           ten years old again
I lie on the grass
and feel the earth move
      as the clouds fly

Eighteen and the old struggles
impinge on my ease
and Frances,
      you have dissolved
           into
                images —
I am an unrealist

The butter-moon floats before us
lights trail across
      shadow water
time-exposed
like comic-strip vibrations
      we turn
           (turn
           ((turn

      Go in
           (in
           ((in and
repeat all the times

      of half-won happiness:
lost again for the future

Myself I would flee
you drift unminding
      in harbours of foreign ships
          a second, or third time,
              a lifetime
coming back
      as if the magic ship
will come for you
      as if the water will snap
into diamond-sea, veins of gold
      you drift back
and I the same
      in foreign waters
      it's all the same
but yes, I do believe
      that the diamond-ships will
          come for us
when we are empty
      Each our own way
      we must go to the desert
where the angels will minister to us.

A DEAD MAN

A man dying is a very little thing —
a name in a newspaper;
there is no hole in the sky
to be plugged up.
It is like taking a cup of sand
from the beach,
it makes a little hole,
you think, somebody
must have trodden it down like that,
and a little boy flattens it out
to build a castle.
Maybe his wife gets a tiny scar
on her heart,
if he had a wife.
Perhaps there is another place
where he goes now.
If there is, it must be
a long way away.
You can never find a man
where he used to be
when he is dead.

FAR AWAY

Far away
in childhood
like England or getting married,
or ships that crawl
so slowly across the horizon,

Some things are
far away,
some hopes are
imprinted on balloons
that float forever away
and disappear painfully
before unflinching eyes.

But wishes seem
to come at us with
the blunt edge of a bumper bar;
the swimmer seems
to turn in the catch
of his last breath,
and it is hard to say
how much he consents
to the closeness of the wave's embrace,
or would struggle to turn
away.

THERE IS NONE THAT SEES TOO FAR

Sunday morning
feeling in the grass for a twig
to toss at the sun,
Jeffrey shields his eyes for a moment
from the exploding myth
but his eyes open stinging:

"I had just begun to see.
Is there no time for the creators?"

"There is none that sees too far
before the day."

There is a moment's reverence
before the impetus of existence
resumes its folly;
if there was a hint of retreat
it is jammed in the past
like the cards that stack
the leg of a table,
and Jeffrey's hands do not reach or grasp.
He is taken to the frontline
where he executes his duty courageously
and turns back the enemy:

"Had I just begun to be,
and is there no time for the creators?"

"There is none that sees too far

before the day."

Jeffrey stands aside
awaiting the outcome:
the captains are deciding
who is to redeem him,
and there will be joy among men
over his repentance,
he will find honour and prosperity
all his days.
Jeffrey hears the priests on a radio
and escapes to a toilet
to write his epitaph.
When he reappears
his dream is wrapped
tightly around him and,
eternity in his eyes,
he dissolves into the texture of futility

"I have just begun to see,
but is there no time for the creators?"

"There is none that sees too far
before the day."

CYNICAL MOMENT

(preamble: a recitation of events:
the observation is the attitude,
the eloquence awaits its moment)

The man with the tie
And his ideas
Will prevail

The young voice raised high
With its jeers
Will fail

The words asking why
And their fears
Will grow stale

The girl with her eyes
Full of tears
Leave no tale

Day ends
With hymn to mankind
With the universe
At the tips of his fingers.

THE SOFT BARRAGE

In the soft barrage of conversations
I take no shape

learning to be docile like the ox
I do not escape

the doors and even the doorways are gone
the earth opens in its seasons

the ox is sold to crueller masters
but heaven wears its reasons

where the water plays out to the depths
I coolly watch

body takes its food
the belt shifts another notch

turning on the tower in the moonlight
all is quiet within

but the message has been delivered already
noticed fastened with a pin:
"You are one layer beneath the skin."

RIVERRUNDOWN
(words of the prophet)

Exuberance, he said, is the flower of youth,
Dignity the crown of age

River run down: the rain on the hills
Cuts its path in the brown earth

Life is found between
Living and being told to live;
The eyes of naivety see only black and white,
But dichotomies fade and hope as well.

River run down: the cool flow on rocks
Reaches the edge of a cliff,
Balances,
free-falls,
dives
down

The man who will endure
Is he who can see the beyond;
The blind stop, and think they have arrived

River run down: majestic
Goddess of crops

Hands, hands that murder and create
And in between fear and darkness
Clutch at something to take away

To remind them of the event,
To hang on the mantle before countless friends —
All as jealous as God.

River run down: into the turbid mouth of the sea

Blessed are the stupid,
For they have the courage to ask
Why.

COMRADES

Again I hear the screaming
see men pinned
where the spotlight is beaming
but there's nowhere to put the words

the comrades have lost out
they carry their chains
and force out their humour
to dull out their pains

and cherish small comforts
to camouflage fear
and don't hear the currents
that pulse in their ears

like it's all just as good
as they'd want it to be
and this white heat of terror
that burns inside me

has no reason to be
has no reason to be

FOND HEARTS

He rides down moonbeams,
she plants smouldering seeds,
together they harvest the waves.

Each time they swim in deeper waters,
calling to silent onlookers
that the sea is deeper than a watching eye,

deeper than calmness suggests,
but there is contentment.
Time which is the constancy of will

scores ever more pathways to the heart,
and the warmth of fond hearts blazes bright
when the winters are savage.

JOY AND SORROW

The other half is happiness,
time as full
as the meaning of a tree
which is a tree which is a tree

words fall away
to leave us inside and outside complete
There is ever so much
ahead
and struggles, lessons

I let go the future
here I
dwell in all fullness

sadness and joy pass
I take it
we are here
the horror, impossibility
of any hope
of any room to exist
in the simple integrity
of earth-flowing manhood

I am the ache
in the heart of all plunderers
but here too
I am
all love

a wedge driven into heaven
drunk on wild pure certainties

the other half is happiness
I am here in happiness
I grin like a fault
in the smooth face of illusions

(gentle should be
the fall into truth)

FOR A CITY FRIEND

You would like it here,
listening to the wind's gentle song,
humming the day long
in the forest's vast horde of leaves,
soft behind the crackling
and piping of birds,
quiet without the concrete and glass
of words.

You would like it here,
the soil is alive in your hands:
crumbling and falling as you turn it,
giving heed to the seed's demand;
and you watch young shoots grow,
(fragile as beginnings are),
wait for their fullness to show.

You would like it here,
crowds, billboards and lies
are at a minimum;
there is wood rotting down
that the loggers didn't take
and you learn
the slow haul of time to heal mistakes.

You would like it here,
the sky performs daily wonders,
surge, billow and high-drift,
the clouds cruise their way swift,

or stand still as trees in last light:
you would want your heart to be this large,
and clear as morning-bright.

BIRTH DAY

Days, months rolled around,
no sharp edges here
but mellow, mellow grew those days;
the world changed
as always
but power was shifting
to the young
who held their scarce dreams
against the onslaught
of the logic of greed

We were there in those days
to see the webs spun,
the paths laid;
we trekked, checked,
held on,
lay still when all else trembled
and knew all small blessings
as signs of triumph,
all children as holy,
each birth another promise of eternity.

FOREST/NIGHT/HOUSE LAMPS

Forest
night
house-lamps

The gilded dragon
turns through sleep
twisting dream-tails
awe-fully.

Forest
night
house-lamps

Moon-ages separate
the weary traveller
from his end
his pillow is a tussock
in the earth's shadow

Forest
night
house-lamps

MING I
Darkening of the Light

Ming I sees the wheel of his life,
clouds steer over the mountain,
as dark as a pit,
but the eternity of his actions
is in the issue of his sincerity:
the light of day is in his love.

Darkness fails to rule —
the proud prince falls in confusion
at his moment of triumph;
the land stirs again:
emptiness awaiting the light.

Ming I turns into the darkness, pure,
empty of false hopes;
he clings to joy like flame to wood:
it is the nature of evil to pass.

THE READING

The pathway to peacefulness
is possible:
through the door of good and evil it lies.
No matter how tightly
the rope has been strained

Seek no path
but to watch the steps that you trace
and the spring will come,
will blossom
in new colours,
so it will be a new vision,
and storm will be calm again.

Let your only act be
the act of the heart
that knows us all as one,
the heart that loves herself
in all whom she encounters.

Across time, walls and strangeness
strive for us all to know
ourselves as one.

Holy, holy, holy,
peace on all paths,
blossoms in eternity.
Time without striving.
Wholly.

IN DANGER

In danger his only protection
is his sincerity;
with confidence he approaches the disturbance,
fulfilling what is necessary
and retreating.
When he is not in demand
he returns to his home;
if you ask him what he does there
it will not seem important.
Perhaps he watches the birds
or puts straw on his garden.

You will hear the sage in hard times —
he is sharpened by adversity.
In victory he will storm through,
flanked, it would seem,
by a dragon horde,
intent on the last crushing blow.
But at once he will turn aside,
and pick his way back silently,
knowing sadness too in that hour.

And one knows
it is only the lesser man
who would stay to mock and plunder.

THE OLD MEN HAVE A SAYING

They read from old books
but do not worship time;
caution they observe
in all their acts.
Who is inspired by their docility?
Soldiers, gypsies or timid men?
Not the timid —
these men know when to move
with flash and fire,
when the right touch will loosen
the spirit's desire;
in crying, laughing,
in silence and in speech
they cling to their inner strength.
What is it they teach
from their old books?
Correctness, and beauty.
The old men have a saying:
Love the One.

THE DRY WELL (Ching)

Water being muddy
the well was abandoned;
dry progress followed.

The last miles at night,
wooden bridges on rough back roads —
then the neat bowl of light,
still and waiting;
coat hung on the door.

Then time for play:
the constant heart is established in joy,
solid at root beneath great trunks
but loose in the wind,
so much so that the crown sways
dangerously,
but he grins,
for his mother is the earth
and he shines
in the mystery of winning
the contest of wind with song.

THE SAGE'S UNDERTAKINGS

If others did as the sage does
their undertakings would proceed
with harmony and excellence.
The sage does not fight with circumstance,
he restrains his wrath
and banishes his fear,
ruling himself with calmness.
He takes his rest
when the mountains withhold his progress;
he moves when the obstacles clear.
In the cast of the mountain's shadow
he does not pronounce doom
but nourishes the secret hope
that hides in the heart of all perils,
retaining his clarity and resilience always.
His silhouette merges with the hills,
a play of light and shadow
dancing in the mysteries of each moment;
effortless is his force.

THE SAGE AS STRANGER

He sees both the desire and its fulfilment,
he knows pain and he knows
its lessons,
he holds no grudge
against necessities.
When he speaks, his conversation is flavoured
sweetly, free of all guile.
He wanders again, a stranger,
walks into places
at delicate times
demanding honesty,
and suddenly is near
(and the world sees)
as the pandemonium clears
and the one spirit
now, in its power,
is.
He stands quietly,
obedient,
forever in command.

KU'N (RECEPTIVE)

The man comes quietly,
he speaks with his heart;
at the foot of the steps he says,
"Father, I am here,"
looks up and is
Ku'n, the Receptive.
To him the Father will speak;
he is a son of the Father
and the Father's good gifts
shower around him.
He does not seek bounty,
nor does he sit and wait for it,
but in following he finds his proper lord.
Ku'n is firm, steady, clear,
a reflector of the Divine Will;
here, and here again,
uncircumscribed by sorrow,
Ku'n is the unbound,
a dancer in the joy of the Lord.

THE LAST SONG

When you have sung the last song
you are empty,
there is not a thought in your reach
that will fill your glass,
for none dare to dwell
in that silence
from which even the echo
of the final chord retreats.

If you would sing your last song,
let it be sung
for other ears than your own,
that their memory may return to you
the love of your voice
dancing on the air,

For if you seal yourself alone,
in the darkness that follows
you will not hear
even the approach of love.

THE LAST SUPPER

Into the room
and he was there and he
washed our feet,
archaic as an angel, God-wise.
What a tangle were our lives —
so many times, it seemed
we had our finger on the truth
and he would shake his head
so much of being up and down
so much of holding onto moments
(days that ached,
altars on the mountain)
so much of standing in the way

Jesus,
is there any chance for us,
we who stand
in the front of crowds
and shout
(yes, we are the ones
who elbowed Zacchaeus);
will we ever become
as small as the flowers
who know the extravagance
of your love?

THE NOTEBOOK

Advancing in emptiness

Although Jesus appears in this poem, it is one of several in this collection that is about me working through the meaning of hexagrams in the *I Ching*, which in turn is echoed in the *Tao Te Ching*.

Margaret, my first wife (1974-1980) introduced me to the *I Ching* and the Tao, and they have been my constant companions ever since. The version I used for many years was the Wilhelm/Baynes edition with the foreword by Carl Jung. Richard Wilhelm intended his translation (from Chinese to German and then into English) to be accessible to the lay Westerner. He built a bridge between the concepts of Chinese philosophy and Christianity, which made it all the more accessible to me, and universalised it for me.

This poem was based on hexagram 31, Influence (wooing) – "the superior man encourages people to approach him by his readiness to receive them". Wilhelm says the mind should be kept humble and free, so that it may remain receptive to good advice. Influence comes from the attraction between heaven and earth – through such attraction the sage influences men's hearts and thus the world attains peace. (The language is as it was in the 1920s.)

This is a poem from my thirties when I was ensconced at Horseshoe Creek.

The badlands

This is not really a poem that cries out for context. If I think about when it was written, it was after Jo-Ann had gone (we had been together off and on for 3-5 years), Rohan was gone with her, and the emotional disarray that was the prelude to her departure was over, leaving a quietness that was both lonely and a relief.

It's easy for me to say I have an inherently melancholy disposition, despite the stupidity of that kind of self-labelling. Yet I have never relinquished a bedrock of optimism. All the good will be. All that, all that. The child will be protected, the destination is the time of release of hopes into wonder.

Images of perfection

I loved my home at Horseshoe Creek. From 1978 to 1983 I worked as a school teacher at St Mary's High School, Casino. It was a lovely time. There was a nice group of teachers, many of whom were around my own age, most of whom were escapees from the city like me. The deputy and the principal were both attuned to the call of Vatican II. As a non-Catholic, I understood this to be a movement within the Catholic Church that was about renewal, in the same way that Michael Newman was. It was characterised by a spirit of openness, social activism and tolerance, a softening of the view that you would only make it into heaven if you took a tough stand on "beliefs". To put it more unkindly, if you were dogmatic.

St Mary's, at that time, was the kind of place that took in kids who had been expelled from the local high school up the road for "bad behaviour", and made them part of the family. There was a huge amount of love in that school.

Soon after I started work there, Margaret left, taking the children with her. I was shocked. We had had twin boys in December 1978, so we had four young kids in all, and day-to-day life was hard, but I was trying hard – I thought *we* were trying hard – and I was totally unprepared for the leaving.

I kept my work-life going, and it was not the sort of thing you talked about with school pupils. And because I lived 30 kilometres away, they were not to know that anything had happened anyway. But they seemed to know. When I was on playground duty at lunchtime, one or two or three of them would come up to me and just talk. There was no real topic of discussion – they would just talk and share stuff with me. And then they'd wander off, when they'd made their offering.

A lot of the time I had the distinct impression that they knew just what they were doing, and it was all about their knowing, whether consciously or unconsciously, that I needed love and support. So without saying anything specific, and perhaps without even knowing anything specific, they were an enormous healing force for me.

Hence, my understanding of this poem is about that time, and still seeing my home as my heartland, and loving coming home.

But here's the twist. The poem was actually written in June 1973. How do I make sense of that? Most of that poem is about the harshness of living up to social images and stereotypes, not feeling good enough, and how you protect yourself. But the frame for that poem is "home" – being that close is a rare gift. Home is the sanctuary.

For me, my home at Horseshoe Creek (Bywater) was the first home of my own. It was where I first put down roots since leaving the home where I grew up. And I stayed there for 20 years, still the longest I've lived anywhere. Does that make sense? "Being that close is a rare gift".

Benjamin woodcutter and the queen

This poem was certainly a thing of wonder to me. It was one of those things that was completed even before it was written down. Quickly. And I didn't have an explanation for it. I don't have any other poems like this one. It's the kind of thing that might alarm psychiatrists.

I have a date for this poem – 24 March 1974. What was happening then? I had had a motor bike accident in January 1973, and spent six months in hospital. The leg was saved and the skin grafts took time. I went back to teaching in October 1973 but resigned in December, which coincided with the expiration of my three-year bond to the New South Wales Department of Education.

I went to work as a psychiatric nurse at Parramatta Psychiatric Centre. I also left home and moved in with Margaret. At the same time I went back to university, aiming to complete my Bachelor of Arts, majoring in Philosophy and Education. And it must have been at the end of March when Elvina was conceived.

So lots of things were going on. The job at the psychiatric centre was about me exploring things I wanted to know about, attempting to understand society and life. The university course was taking a messy turn. The philosophy department at Sydney University was embroiled in a war between the traditionalists, the existentialists and the Marxists. The education department had chosen anarchy as its expression of liberation and wasn't teaching anything.

I remember that I quit university at the end of March. The other factor at this time was that my mother was traumatised by my leaving home. When I had first mentioned to her that I wanted to move out, she had not spoken for a week. I was not equipped to weather that kind of heaviness. Her husband, my father, had died when I was sixteen. My sister and brother had since moved away, and I was the only one left at home.

Perhaps this information makes the poem crystal clear.

Wanting

There is a precise date for this poem. 8 April 1973. In January I had had a motor bike accident. My right leg was badly damaged, and there was one week in February when I was facing the prospect of losing the leg because of gangrene. Miraculously, the gangrene disappeared. I went into the operation to have the bottom half of the leg amputated, and there was no more gangrene. Mmmm.

One of my memories of that day is of one of the nurses, who came into the ward an hour before I went into the operation with a huge bunch of tiger lilies. "For strength," she said. Tears in her eyes, tears in mine.

Once I stabilised after the operation, I was moved from Western Suburbs Hospital to Royal Prince Albert Hospital to have skin grafts to cover the gaping hole in my leg.

By early April the skin graft process had commenced. It involved cutting up a section of skin from my hip and sewing it onto my wrist for six weeks before then grafting it onto my leg (another six weeks), then releasing it from my wrist. There were eight operations in all.

Given that I had faced losing my leg, I figured I could summon the patience to go through the skin graft process. *Wanting* is about the underlying bliss that enables and feeds patience.

A dark day then

Ah, where is Chrissie now? Chrissie was from my innocent days in the Anglican church fellowship at Greenacre (circa 1965-1971 for the historians). It was the peak time of church fellowships in the suburbs of Sydney. I was the leader of the group, and there were up to 60 people who turned up on Sunday evenings, to sing songs, have Bible studies, conduct philosophical discussions and compare clothes and musical preferences (Beatles, Rolling Stones, Elvis Presley or the burgeoning group of artists that the advent of the Beatles had unleashed – and then there was the US San Francisco phenomenon).

It was all exciting, but we had all grown up in the Australian suburbs, Bob Menzies' suburbia of the 1960s. We lived comfortably inside a paradigm. Key elements were Victa mowers and the June Dally-Watkins School of Deportment. We did not know what paradigms were, or that there might be other paradigms. That realisation came bumpily, through people who blundered outside the straightened way. Like Chrissie.

Chrissie had bliss inside her waiting to break out. Along with it, she had a multitude of demons. And she was extremely sensual. At a time when I was dutifully constrained by Christian virtue. I was older, and she looked up to me. But along with that, there was the motor bike, a vehicle of sensuality. We spent many hours together on my motor bike (the Yamaha 180, the Honda 450), she on the back and huddled up close, us weaving through curved roads or sailing along country highways.

Times. There was one time when she turned up at my place late at night, out of her mind, distraught. And in possession of a small quantity of white powder. In about 1969. We were all so innocent. What was this white powder? We hadn't even come across marihuana. She allowed me to flush it down the sink, but she was wrung out, and I spent an hour riding around looking for a chemist that was open, hoping for what? An antidote? A cure? An answer?

Another time I was at teachers' college, at lectures on a sunny autumn day in a place that had apotheosised irrelevance. I received a message from the office (hand-delivered) that I was needed to see Chrissie. I had no idea why, and I was young. How do you explain walking out of a lecture where there are only a dozen people present? And it was so formal, the college admin person taking a phone message and walking over to the classroom.

I got on my motor bike and went to her place. She was just scattered. Wanting to take the powder, take the pills, possessed by that irritable energy. What was I supposed to do? I just talked, ill-equipped, not understanding and probably not much help.

The next day at college I had to explain my absence. I had to submit a form. I didn't know how to accomplish that. Fortunately the lady in the office knew. She said there was a formula – it was called "urgent personal business". So that was it.

A dark day is not a description of Chrissie. As I said, there was bliss underneath. It is a description of my frustration, my inability to comprehend or know what to do. Years later, she turned up at a place I used to go to. I was taking another girl out at the time, and Chrissie turned up. And I was giving them both a lift home. In a car this time.

Who was going to go first? It was Chrissie, and she couldn't believe it. But why not? I was going out with the other girl at the time. Beyond this point, things could get ugly. There could be a conversation about doubt. And there could be a conversation about being sensible (around a girl who used drugs).

I stop that with a position statement about not harbouring regrets.

Paint me a picture

I'm starting to believe the theory about melancholy. Then again, poems are like prayers – they're more likely to happen when you're in trouble, and need to make sense of adversity. So I reach for the record that tells me when it was written. October 1972.
So. I'm getting protective. I'm not saying who this was. It was a friendship, and indeed, still is. It had been, was, is still, important. If friends reside in circles, this was one of the inner circles. My early twenties was a torrid time. Not that I'm claiming excessive suffering. By no means. I think that's a torrid period for anyone – lots of changes, shifts, decisions, directions to take. Standing on one's own feet, tentatively, clumsily.

Roselle, new friend, says I should own my own experience, and not hide behind generalities. Okay, no hiding. I felt myself shifting ground with my friend. We were both changing, we were both figuring out what we wanted in life, and from other people, and from each other. Was it comfort, exploration, freedom from judgement? And in what areas of life? She was doing the intense household thing – "total honesty" with four others day by day, clothes on, clothes off, while I was trying to construct a new world by formulating a more soundly based Christian creed, writing articles and giving talks to church groups.

Somewhere else I talk about the distinction between wanting and needing. Did I want her friendship, or did I need it? Was I "using" her to meet my need? And was I outgrowing my need, so can you look at this poem cynically? Agh, my head hurts.

And all this happens in dance time. I move my feet, you move yours. Sometimes we tread on each other's feet. There is one line in the poem that may be unfair, from my current vantage point – "have you withdrawn your pledge?" Just what, exactly, can we pledge between friends? I think of battered wives, and if I were a battered wife, I would leave. We can't pledge the future, because the only thing we should commit to is to be true to ourselves.

I think of people I have chosen to separate from, since that time, and my conscious choice has been to cut free because they withdrew *their* pledge. The pledge in any relationship, whether it is friendship, marriage or another kind of partnership, is to love the other. What this means may change over time, and it's also difficult to disentangle want and need. Nevertheless, love is easy enough to understand, and keeping one's focus on that tends to shape reality profitably.

And I think I knew even then that my friend had not withdrawn *that* pledge.

Yellow smoke on the water

This poem follows the previous for this reason. I had many people who came to visit me in hospital over those six months. Some of them visited in faithfulness, regularly. Some of them visited occasionally. Even that was good – I was a hungry man.

Frances came occasionally. She had a boyfriend, and another life from mine. She was somewhat of a mystery to me, but there was a generous soul there.

After I came out of hospital, there was a gnawing wasteland when I was at home and helpless. I couldn't ride a bike or drive a car. I wasn't ready to go back to work. So I was challenged by the aridness of the routines of the invalid's home life. Before the bike accident I had been actively involved in a Christian centre called the House of the New World, a hothouse of ferment that mirrored the secular upheavals in young society. Now I was marooned.

Sometimes, someone would take me out. Frances came one day and we went down to a beach south of Sydney. An afternoon became evening. Hospital had retarded numerous personal developments, and only recently I had been (finally) introduced to marihuana. *Yellow smoke on the water* is fuelled by an early experience of the effects of cannabis.

I really appreciated marihuana. It opened doors, it raised questions, it offered new ways of looking at situations in which I had felt imprisoned, and it released wellsprings of feeling and insight. Sometimes when I have written something and have felt inspired in doing so (gathered up), I think that what I have written is wiser than me. There is still something really powerful to me about "each our own way, we must go to the desert, where the angels will minister to us".

That may sound indulgent or arrogant. That's an inherent danger of this exercise. But in any case, I'm merely saying that what I write is meaningful to me. Somewhere else I wrote (maybe it's in the next volume), "My wisdom is mine alone". There is no guru, there are no disciples. There is experience to share, that's my invitation.

A dead man

My father died when I was 16. He was 53. It was sudden. One afternoon. It was an unusual day – I was working with him to replace the roof on the "temporary dwelling". There are so many stories here already. In the early 1950s, Sydney was still suffering from shortages of materials, post-World War II. It was difficult to get a house built, and after the war there were so many more families – reunited families with returned soldiers, and migrants from Europe.

Accommodation was at a premium. My parents married in 1947, and they lived in other people's houses until they bought the block of land at Greenacre in August 1954. My four-year-old mind remembered that date. The block of land was covered with bush, the road was dirt, and there was a "temporary dwelling" on it, a thirty-foot by twelve-foot fibro, one-room building with a lean-to on the side that had a bath and laundry tubs.

Mum and dad and us three kids lived in that building until I was nine. We moved into the house in May 1959 (that date was painted in black script by the painter in the top corner of the external wall at the back). During those years there was a war with the local council about these temporary dwellings. The council took the view that they were substandard and people shouldn't be living in them. Easy enough to say.

My mum has reminded me that she and dad went to a meeting in Bankstown with about 300 others to protest about the council's intolerant and unrealistic policy. The talk of evictions was just cranking up stress levels for people who had no means to do other than what they were doing. No one was living in a dump by choice.

Our little scenario was lived out by countless others during the fifties and early sixties in what was then the western suburbs, the outskirts of Sydney. The dream was to build a nice house, make it a home, and have a lovely garden. Mum and dad did that. We had a huge block of land, and mum and dad created a neat, beautiful garden. It was picturesque.

The temporary dwelling stayed. Its existence was never questioned. First, mum's niece and her new husband lived in it for three years while they were building their house out at Lugarno. After that, Brian (my brother) and I took possession of it. We were allowed to paint it. We had a table tennis table, and spent hours playing table tennis there during our teen years. It was my study and his. I had a table and a cupboard, and dad bought me a typewriter. Ah, magic.

But it got to the point where the roof leaked, so dad and mum decided to replace the corrugated iron. It was all organised. Measurements taken, materials purchased and delivered, a power drill organised (we owned nothing of that nature). My main thing in those days was study. I was aiming for high marks in the Higher School Certificate so that I could get to university. I would be the first person in the Martin family to do so (there was a lot of underlying mythology here, both an inspiration and a burden).

There was a serious conversation between mum and me. She said I had to put my study aside this weekend. I had to help dad. And I was obedient. I didn't fight about it. I said okay. Dad and I had not spent a lot of time together since I started high school. Before that we used to go to soccer games together on Saturdays. That was when Australia first started to invite overseas clubs to visit. Dad and I saw English, Italian, Greek and Spanish teams play. It was exciting, as well as being my first real experience of other cultures in the crowds.

I think the job of replacing the roof daunted dad. He was a painter, not a builder. I vaguely remember he had some help from neighbours. I was there, doing what I could. Given my focus on matters of the intellect, I was pretty much useless at practical skills. And I had a perfectionist bent that focused too much on detail – like trying to get a margin of error of one in 10,000 when one in ten would do just fine.

The day was going alright. Old sheets were coming off and new sheets were going on. The screws and nails were working out okay, and the sheets seemed to be staying straight and covering what they needed to. About two o'clock, dad got pains in the chest. He seldom got sick and I never thought about him being sick beyond an occasional cold.

He went and lay on his bed and mum called the doctor. Everything was big in those days – we didn't have a phone, so ringing a doctor meant asking a favour from a neighbour. The doctor came, and dad seemed okay. The doctor said he should rest. Which was alarming, as we still had parts of the roof that were uncovered, and what if it rained? I had assumed some sense of responsibility by now, I wasn't just passing the nails and screws and obeying orders.

The doctor was packing his bag to go when dad had the heart attack. The doctor said to get him down on the floor, and told me to help him to do resuscitation. He did the pushing on the chest and told me to breathe air into his mouth strongly– now, pause, now, pause, now. That's right. Keep it up. Mum was told to call the ambulance. Back to the neighbours.
Dad was dead. He'd gone, just like that. I was breathing air into the lungs of someone who had already gone. Around eight o'clock that night (maybe), mum and I were sitting in

the visitors' room at Bankstown Hospital and the doctors finally came and said what we already knew. They hadn't been able to revive him. We got home somehow.

Most of the details escape me. Who drove us home? We had no car. Where was Brian? I know that Helen, my older sister, was away for the weekend at some kind of camp, and someone had to go and get her and bring her home. I know that Brian cried for a week. And mum cried, but she was also faced with the fear of not being able to keep things going. There was a mortgage. There were such powerful fears afoot. It was as if the grief was overshadowed by these fears.

What assailed me the most? I was the central character in the "going to university" mythology. I was the one who was going to succeed in that way. I was in Year 12, my final year of school. So – would I have to leave school, and get a job in a shop or an office to earn money to keep the household going? Would this spell the end of a lifetime's aspiration (as vague as it was)?

Then combine this with my guilt over my selfishness. I was paralysed. The result? Numbness. I felt numb for ages. Mum swallowed her sadness, talked to the bank and social security, and sorted it out, so she could keep it all going, with me and Brian at school. I was okay most of the time. The thing that brought me unstuck was people's sympathy.
At the funeral, there were lots of pupils there from school. There were probably 200 people in that tiny weatherboard church at Greenacre, St David's. I thought I was okay, being strong for mum. No tears. Listening to the words, keeping

my perspective, not falling into that emotional pit from which I might not return. But outside the church, one of my school friends came up to me and touched me on the shoulder and said, "Sorry." I went to pieces then. For a short time.

I got an image for it later. Dad dying was like a wall being removed from the house. You don't think about a wall being removed. But it's gone, and you think, the roof can't possibly stay up.

In those days I was writing a lot of poetry. The travail and explorations of that period of life. (I don't like that sentence, but let it stay. I just don't like being trite about "periods of life". We can experience anything anytime, especially when we wake up and choose to.) But I didn't write anything about dad. It was a case of – let's not talk about the wall that just disappeared. Let's just hope the roof stays up. And perhaps it will if we don't talk about it.

I wrote "A dead man" in November 1970, three and a half years later. I accept that many people might find this totally unsatisfactory as a poem about the death of one's father. I'm sorry. This poem is my tears for my father. I sat down and faced his death. There's a lot that the poem doesn't say. That feeling I had that I had not appreciated him or acknowledged him during his life. What he had given up in providing for all of us. The fact that he died so young.

Well, it's implicit. When I wrote the poem, the overriding thing still was the suddenness of his death, and the fact that life went on without him.

Here's a strange experience. It's not even directly about me. Many years later, Lois, to whom I was married for a decade, visited a clairvoyant. Curiously, the clairvoyant spent part of the time talking about me and Margaret, my first wife. What was said is not relevant here. The curious thing was, the clairvoyant's "informant" was my father. I thought it was rather cheeky of a clairvoyant to discuss matters other than those to do with the person in the room.

So when this was related to me, I realised that it was all okay – my father had loved me, and had forgiven, or overlooked, my youthful conceits.

Far away

This was written in September 1970. The significance of that is minimal. When I wrote this, there was an immediate circumstance, but I also had in mind the general concept of finally getting something you sought, but when it actually arrives you experience doubts about whether you really want it.

There is none that sees too far

This was written in July 1971. I said (or inferred) above that I wrote regularly for a long period of time. That is, I wrote most days, most weeks. Yet there was a period of several months when I was estranged from the discipline, perhaps most of a year. Some of that was about love (undiscovered or unrequited) and some of it was about being stuck about work, career or the direction of my life generally.

I remember that when Bob Dylan was running hot in the early days, his output was prodigious. Some weeks he wrote up to ten songs.

This poem was the first I wrote after a long period of drought. Jeffrey is an invention. There are two reference points for this. One is my fifth grade teacher, Mr James, at Bankstown North Primary School. They were the days of large classes, close to 40 pupils. There were seldom any spare seats in the classroom. In fifth grade there was only one. Mr James, a mild-mannered man, invariably in a double-breasted light grey suit, invented Wilbur, who occupied the spare seat.

Sometimes he would address Wilbur instead of us, and sometimes Wilbur had qualities that the rest of us couldn't muster, but we all liked Mr James, and we always felt he was teaching us.

And I have a vague memory of Ian Anderson, in Jethro Tull, the wild man with his flute, inventing such a character. Perhaps it was even Jeffrey. So Jeffrey has pedigree. He can carry the load.

The early seventies were the days of exploding myths, and mythologies. I saw most of the bulwarks and mainstays of my upbringing as being candidates for explosion. That idea, that certitude, oops, all wrong, all barren. The new myth that was characterised in one mode by cannabis (à la San Francisco 1968) was exposing tame suburban predictability as a sell-out of what was possible.

At the same time, the Vietnam war was creating an extremely ugly reality as a consequence of the dominant paradigm (I think the saying, "the dominant paradigm" had not yet made its appearance in 1971, but was soon to do so.). This is why Jeffrey goes to "the frontline", although the other frontline was the psychiatric centre.

In this poem, the suburban dream that my parents (particularly my mum) had tried to create is given its death warrant. I looked to the possibility of creativity. I saw the suburbs as an insidious prison. Later I expanded my view – I decided that it wasn't that the suburbs were inherently wrong. Rather, it was the idea that that's *all* there was that was the problem. It was the placing of a ceiling over the reality and saying, "This is what you can aspire to", meaning "this is the utmost you can aspire to".

Jeffrey hangs on to eternity, and good for him.

Cynical moment

This is not a whole poem, it is the last part of a long harangue. I've spared you that ordeal. It dates from July 1970. I was prolific that year. Why did I select this poem for inclusion? Because it is indicative of a basic theme of mine at this time – wrestling with the idea that life is a matter of learning a social role and assuming it. Being original or free or creative is looked upon disparagingly. Indeed, it is generally crushed by the prevailing forces of convention. And this is allied with a huge conceit, that humanity is progressing and has already achieved greatness, and the only task is to defend it against usurpers and naysayers.

I am importuned to believe that this is a thread in the Martin family, that is, what we might call social dissonance – "we" always see ourselves in opposition to the mainstream. This is not to say that I believe that. I don't hold a process view about social dissonance. I think that I was born at the right time (it was 1950). Whatever happened after that wasn't a process, it was an event. Which is to say, social dissonance is not always relevant, but sometimes it is.

"Day ends with hymn to mankind..." The event was the prevalence of human arrogance. As if humans could deny their reliance on nature. As if it was okay to chop down trees simply because they were there and they were big. As if humans could dig up coal forever. I never understood all that. (Still don't.)

The soft barrage

Again, I start with the date: June 1974. Margaret was pregnant with Elvina; I had left university and high school teaching, and was working as a psychiatric nurse at Parramatta Psychiatric Centre. I was thinking about writing, the direction of my life, and I had started using the I Ching.

The ox crops up in the I Ching as a symbol of docility. In this poem I was trying out docility, as a way of finding my way.

I wasn't expecting to get "there" suddenly, just to get closer. I do not think it is easy to be docile like the ox. It can get confused with passivity, apathy or cowardice.

Riverrundown

September 1970. I was at Sydney Teachers' College and had started studying for an Arts degree (which I abandoned in the third year). Even if things weren't ideal, at least I had moved closer to dealing with myself as a writer rather than as a victim who had to spend his life doing alien work.

I had spent the previous two years studying civil engineering at the University of New South Wales, a huge mistake. The decision to do engineering was a product of my lack of confidence and my lack of ideas about a career of my choosing. As the first in my family to go to university, the range of ideas about what I would do at university was somewhat narrow.

The family history extended to teachers and nurses. I was keen to be a little more innovative. "Everyone" told me that it would be better to do a science-based course rather than an arts-type course. "You'll always be able to get a job as an engineer."

In Maslow's hierarchy of human needs, safety and security constitute the second of five levels. So choosing to study engineering was a Level 2 decision, far short of self-esteem or self-actualisation. I hadn't been able to bring myself to ask the next question: What would be the point if you weren't happy?

This was the general context, but it doesn't explain the poem. And I wonder why I ran the words together like that. It was a Gerard Manley Hopkins touch. I had been much enamoured of his poetry in Year 12. There was an explosive excitement about what he did with words, and running the words together was one of the things he would have done, as a kind of alliterative joke. At this point in time, it is amusing that running words together is a necessity imposed by the internet when formulating website addresses.

And how do I explain the content of the poem? It was about trying to get a grasp, as a young man, on the concept of wisdom. I was acknowledging – I am young, I am ignorant, but I hope to grow, I hope to understand, and I think this must unfold the same way as a river forms and takes shape in the mountains, and passes through phases and one day empties into the sea as a mighty river that humanity calls significant.

The other aspect of this poem I remember is that I was writing for Margaret, I was wanting her to see that my writing was something of value, and so was I. I showed it to her, of course, and I didn't see that she thought anything at all about it. No judgement, just the reality.

Comrades

I left teaching in January 1974 and took up psychiatric nursing. Several fellow pupils from high school had trod the same path. For me it was about exploring the psychology of humans, and the workings of society. In my late teens and early twenties I was possessed by a zeal to understand everything, from people and society to the cosmos, religions, politics and the spirit world.

I thought that psychiatric institutions were a flash point for society. They were a place where the forces that societal authority commands are used to bludgeon dissent and mysteries into submission. And the inmates were casualties, people who were unwittingly threats to the prevailing conceptions of what was an acceptable (ie tame, mindless, received, unquestioning) life.

Around this time there were a few poems that I sent to various poetry magazines. This was one of them. They were all rejected, accompanied by various comments intended to be gently disparaging. It was Les Murray (at *Poetry Australia*) who said he really objected to the repetition of the last line. I didn't – I thought it was necessary, and I am unrepentant.

Working at Parramatta Psychiatric Centre affected me a lot. I worked most of the time in a lock-up ward with 20-foot high sandstone walls, just like Parramatta Gaol down the road. Many of the inmates had been there since the early 1950s. Many of those were casualties of lobotomies and ECT (electro-convulsive "therapy"). I spent a lot of time reading patients' files.

I thought that this was the real, the ugly, under-belly of society. You only understand society when you know all the things it does to deal with all the things it can't cope with – crime, "madness" and household waste. I wasn't presuming to try to understand everything and everyone. However, I looked at specific people there and wondered about them.

To take one of these men (I worked mostly in male-only wards), my understanding was that he had come to Australia from Europe after the war. He had been a young man, he had probably seen and suffered awful things. He was moved around several times after he arrived, and he started a job in Sydney. He started behaving in disturbing ways. It didn't seem that any of this behaviour was extreme, or threatening to other people, but he was placed in the psychiatric centre.

From there on it went downhill quickly. He obviously didn't "respond" well to his treatment, and he was given ECT many times. My sense was that when he started settling down in Sydney, with a place to live and a job, the memories of the war came back and wanted to be faced and put to rest.

People around him weren't ready to deal with that. They did not understand the circumlocutory ways in which the psyche can work, and the odd ways in which feelings and memories can surface. And nor did the psychiatrists. Their concern was social conformism. ECT was their latest weapon in the struggle to make people behave normally.

You realise that half the words in this section should have quotation marks around them – they are loaded terms. I read Thomas Szasz's book, *The myth of mental illness,* at this time. It presented the concept of mental illness as a way of being that people choose when conditions of living have become intolerable, and conversely, psychiatry as a way of managing people who are presenting us with ideas we do not want to face as a society.

In this man's case, I think there were two issues that were too hard for the people around him in the early 1950s – facing his pain, which meant learning and coming to terms with the horrors he had experienced, and understanding the odd ways in which the pain manifested.

I'm not presenting this as science (quotation marks), merely (more quotation marks) as the picture I developed from watching the man's behaviour, reading the notes, and listening to the male nurses who had been there since the fifties. Most of them were harsh and cruel. When I had the courage to ask the meanest one, who was head of the ward, to explain what had happened to this man, he explained it this way:
"He had a mental disturbance. That happens with some people. He was mentally sick. ECT cleaned out people's heads and got rid of all the bad stuff. The job then was to reprogram their heads so they could live a normal life. The reason that didn't work was because the reprogramming wasn't done well enough. Reprogramming was just a matter of getting them to learn a set of behaviours."

I saw that attitude result in a great deal of brutality in the ward. Violence was regular. And I saw young people come in, fresh from home, and who were behaving in ways that I would call confused, but not completely detached from their surroundings. With the standard treatment of drugs and beatings for any non-passive behaviour, they quickly learned how to survive. None of it had anything to do with sanity or mental health.

[2007: I read some reviews of Szasz's book on Amazon.com. Szasz's position is summed up in this quote:
"The reclassification of non-illnesses as illnesses has, of course, been of special value to physicians and to psychiatry as a profession and social institution. The prestige and power of psychiatrists have been inflated by defining ever more phenomena as falling within the purview of their discipline."

The opinions on Szasz's perspective were, as I might have expected, polarised. Three examples are:
1. "In the 1960's facing the cruel conditions of institutionalization and coercive psychiatry, writers such as R.D. Laing, Ken Kesey and Thomas Szasz commented on real oppression but took a swerve in the opposite direction. As a person with mental illness, I cannot agree with what Thomas Szasz is saying."
2. "When I was a psychology major, Szasz's views made for interesting conversation. Having been diagnosed with major depressive disorder, and later having worked as a mental health advocate, his views are punitive and cruel. How sad that fascinating often outweighs truth."
3. "This book is as needed as ever in our present age of "biological" psychology, where general practitioners who know little to nothing about psychology are quick to prescribe drugs in order to medicate the patient into a stupor sufficiently hazy enough that s/he will not care about the

presenting symptoms, all the while wholly ignoring the underlying behavioral causes of the turmoil and dissatisfaction."]

I think the person who reviewed the poem for the magazine thought I was being melodramatic. I wasn't. I was writing out a sense of helplessness about something I was seeing every day and which I felt was extremely wrong. The arrogance of the psychiatrists there was supreme, and most of the ones I came across acted heartlessly. I was probably naïve, but I thought that most of the problems were about wounded hearts, and compassion might have done a lot of good.

I lasted not much longer than six months as a psychiatric nurse. I had seen enough. I took it as a symptom of a sick society. I wanted to get away, and I was thinking about alternative societies and the bush.

Fond hearts

April 1976. Margaret and I are living in Mackay, Queensland. After Elvina was born, in November 1974 in Sydney, I applied for a teaching job in Mackay. It was a way of getting away from Sydney, a stepping stone towards an alternative life, towards finding an alternative community. That was the dream – to find a community. The first Nimbin festival had happened, but I was never attracted to Nimbin.

I think that when we left Sydney, I just wanted to get as far away as possible. I had found teaching hard – I looked at it as a machine that taught children how to conform. But teaching was my only means of earning an income. (I am saying this now from the vantage point of having since taken on a wide range of jobs successfully. I had no ideas or enough bravery then.)

In April 1976, I was still teaching in Mackay. It was not as volatile as the western suburbs of Sydney, so life was a bit calmer that way. The education system seemed staid and moribund. A few outsiders were unsettling things a bit. It was the mid-seventies when there was a teaching shortage Australia-wide, and teachers were being recruited from overseas.

Among my close friends at school were teachers from England and the United States. None of us were outrageous, but all of us were different enough to question the wisdom or value of some of the school's practices. This was discomforting to the principal and to teachers who had been there a long time. They were not used to questioning ideas. This was Queensland during the Joh Bjelke-Petersen era. There was an accepted way and anyone who thought differently must be some kind of criminal or pervert. And they knew how to deal with people like that.

I had seen the film, *Easy Rider*, in Sydney a couple of years earlier. Mackay at the time Margaret and I were there was the kind of place that made the film credible, and paranoia a perfectly sensible attitude. It was in one sense a friendly place, but only on certain conditions. If it was suspected you didn't subscribe to their world view (which was the only world view), you were treated with suspicion.

This poem has nothing to do with societies or communities….. It's about a relationship. Yes, true. Nevertheless, my dream was of this kind of relationship, lovely, sitting within an alternative community that was loving and open, not judging and conforming. The relationship at this point is about the consolation of one another when the social context is not welcoming. The allusion is in the last line: "when the winters are savage".

A footnote: I remember a conversation at Horseshoe Creek in 1979 where I was talking with Margaret and one of the neighbours, and I was talking about the importance of fondness in relationships. The neighbour thought it was a weak way to see relationships. She said there had to be more, and of course she was alluding to passion. But I wasn't dismissing passion.

When I put the pieces together now, I recall that I later learned that that lady had been having an affair at that time with someone. And I think that her husband was fond of her….. and perhaps that was all. And it was the following year that Margaret left me. This is not giving fondness a good name.

Nevertheless! Last word – the I Ching talks about relationships. It boldly says that marriages are based on affection and tact. Affection = fondness. This is a very challenging viewpoint. What about passion? My view? I think a lasting relationship has to be about love that is vast. Part of that vastness is flexibility – there are times when different qualities are called for. I still agree with the I Ching, that affection (fondness) is central. Think of affection as an abiding feeling, one that is tended constantly, a big field in which more particular feelings also reside – and among these, passion.

I'm sure a lot of people are challenged by the idea that people need to exercise tact within a relationship, although many people acknowledge it to be true. They may think it is patronising, and that it suggests you are not really close. Just think, we are all slow learners, we all still have egos that get bruised easily. When we are indeed wise, we will need the tact of our partners less often – when we swim in deeper waters.

Joy and sorrow

Late June 1974. Margaret and I married in early June, an "alternative" wedding in a backyard at Denistone, the minister being Trevor Hulme, who was a Baptist minister, but one who had become involved with the House of the New World at West Ryde. We were all explorers then.

Margaret and I were living in a house in Meadowbank, that the real estate agent said was going to be demolished soon, so they could only give us a short lease. It was an old brick house with an overgrown backyard. It was across the road from the railway line, the main line going north. At 3 o'clock in the morning the goods train would rumble through on its way to Brisbane, so loudly you thought it was coming into the room. You can just see the house from the train, still (in 2007). They never did tear it down.

It was here that I had my first garden, in a space cleared of knee-high kikuyu grass. In some ways I was unhinged – I had left teaching after three years, I knew I was only going to be a psych nurse for a short time, I was doing casual teaching at various schools to make some extra dollars, and I was thinking about getting out of Sydney, finding a place in the bush. And Margaret was pregnant, so it seemed to make sense to make a move before the child (who turned out to be Elvina) was born.

And we did move. We left Sydney in January 1975 for Mackay, Queensland. I had obtained a position as a mathematics teacher at Mackay North High School. We would treat this as our first step towards a place in the country.

Joy and sorrow? They co-existed. I had reason to be happy. My sorrow was about dissatisfaction – with myself, not knowing what to do, not wanting to be a teacher, not liking the way schools were, or psych centres, or churches. And not seeing a pathway to use writing as my livelihood; not seeing how to express self and make a living. Caught in the tangle of that.

Was leaving Sydney and wanting a place in the country escapism? Easy to say yes. But. There was an idealism there, and I'm not sorry about that. I see it in my children too, a kind of idealism that refuses to give it up in order to be "sensible" and tread the trodden path. I think Margaret eventually tired of the burrows I dug in order to pursue this idealism. I think she wanted a more normal life, not the house ten miles out of town at Horseshoe Creek.

And of course, the pursuit of idealism seldom comes without baggage, the baggage of mistaken beliefs and family characteristics, flaws, weights. Easier sometimes for other people to see that side. That too another trap – self-punishment. Hence: "gentle should be the fall into truth".

For a city friend

Sometime in 1977. Margaret and I had been to Mackay, where we lasted 18 months. Mackay at that time was a big sugar town. Farmers were still busy clearing vast tracts of treed landscape for more cane. Two bulldozers in parallel, maybe 50 metres apart, and a huge chain between them. It was amazing what that arrangement could do to open forest in one afternoon. We would drive out to somewhere on a picnic, and when we came back near dusk, there was the smell of raw earth and a lunar vista, bare to the horizon. A huge pile of brush at one end. In a week it would be burning. In a month it would be ploughed and planted.

We went from there to the far north coast of New South Wales, and after some time on a multiple occupancy on 600 acres at the top of the McKellar Ranges west of Lismore we found ourselves living in a farmhouse west of Kyogle, one step away from hippie-land.

At McKellar Range we had lived in a big tent for six months, her and I and Elvina and Holly. I had a big old Land Rover. It took 20 minutes to drive up to our site from the floor of

Rock Valley where the road to town was. There was no power and no water. I used to fill a 44-gallon drum with water and bring it up in the Land Rover.

Although the property was a multiple occupancy, it was nothing like a hippie commune. There were half a dozen other families, couples and singles stationed in their own spots spread over the 600 acres. They had bush encampments like ours – a tent or a caravan, and a lean-to shelter of bush poles and corrugated iron roof, and a dirt floor and a fireplace where the cooking was done.

One couple was soft and spiritual. Another couple was more into art, creativity and grass. Another family consisted of an ex-Vietnam veteran, his Philippino wife, and two young sons. There was a single guy whose thing was gardening. Occasionally there were meetings, and talks about doing things communally. Not a lot of that nature happened. There were a few parties and gatherings.

Margaret found it too tough and too isolated. I was frustrated because I didn't have the money to do the things I wanted to. I wanted to build a house, set up water and a slow-combustion stove, fence a garden area. I wanted goats, and I did get a nice Saanen goat which I learned to milk. That wasn't easy either. Sometimes she was fine, and other days she was cantankerous.

And I was trying to do everything, learn everything. I had never been "practical" while growing up. I had thought of myself as an intellectual, so I wasn't good with hammers or saws or spanners. And I didn't want to get a job to earn money. I had the dream of self-sufficiency.

Leaving McKellar Range was difficult for me because it was an admission of failure. I had so wanted the dream to work, and I wasn't able to.

I had never heard of Kyogle, but the ex-Vietnam vet had lived over that way and he suggested I have a look. So I visited.

I stopped at the top of the pass on the Murwillumbah Road. The lookout was called Durham Lookout. Our house in Mackay had had a coloured glass plaque which pronounced it to be Durham House. I looked down into the valley. Kyogle was a small town off to the left. The land in front of me was farm land – Fawcetts Plains – with crops and cows. Off to the right were the mountains that were renamed in the early 1980s as the Border Ranges, with The Helmet as the first point of prominence.
The country was more bush than rainforest. I liked it. I had found the forests closer to the coast a bit too heavy and close. I went to a real estate agent and he had a house for rent on a cattle property about 20 kilometres west of Kyogle. That was Wyndham Creek.

We moved there in January 1977. I always seem to move at the beginning or end of the year. The house had power and water, a weatherboard house that was probably 50 years old. Later we were told that the house had been moved three times in its life, first up the road about a mile, and then down the other way a mile or two, using bullock drays.

The house was near to a larger house where the caretakers of the property lived, old Sam Nicolls and Mrs Nicolls. The farm was owned by a chemist in town, and we became friends with him. John was a curiosity – and he thought we were curious too.

John's father had been a chemist before him, same shop in Kyogle. John was a few years older than me, and still single. He had a girlfriend, a good Catholic woman who taught infants school. They had been odd companions for years. She also led the marching girls each year in the Fairymount Festival parade. Red and white uniforms, if I recall correctly, and she, of course, carried a baton, which must still be leaning against a cupboard wall in her bedroom.

When the local Fairymount Festival was on, all the shops would enter into the spirit of it (Kyogle had one main street) and they would dress up. I remember that year that John had all his shop-girls dressed up as Playboy bunnies. I was bemused.

John had been brought up in Kyogle, which was a conventional cattle, dairy and timber town. But he was curious about the hippie thing. I took him up to McKellar Range one day and showed him the garden I'd had there – I was still picking vegetables off it months after I'd moved to Wyndham Creek.

When I told him I wanted a garden at Wyndham Creek, he got hold of a big tractor-mounted rotary hoe and ploughed up a quarter of an acre for me. He let me scrounge around for fence posts and old wire, and put up a fence around it.

I didn't have a job until towards the end of that year, and I created the best garden, even through the winter when we had frost almost every day for two months. I grew silver beet that was waist-high, enormous cabbages, and beautiful root vegetables – carrots, parsnips, beetroots.

I entered lots of my vegetables in the Kyogle Agricultural Show, and won several prizes:
> Beetroot, three, large – First Prize
> Cabbage, small – First Prize
> Collection of seasoning herbs, green – First Prize
> Eschallots, one bunch, small – Second Prize
> Collection of vegetables, 12 or more varieties – Second Prize.

What a splendid laugh that was.

1977 was really a "taking time out" year. I'd had decent gardens before – at Mackay and McKellar Range – but this one was better. I had space, time and water. The garden at McKellar Range had done well, but only because the rain had been kind. At Wyndham Creek I learned the right times of the year for different vegetables, and I had the time to weed and fertilise and mulch.

I had good crops and I took boxes of vegetables into the health food shop in town to sell.

It was an in-between time. We were looking around for a place to buy, and we bought the place at Horseshoe Creek in December. It was also an in-between time in terms of work. I was on the dole. Around October, I got a job teaching at St Mary's High School in Casino, and I stayed there for five years.

The girls liked it at Wyndham Creek. I have a lovely photo of them on a frosty morning, acres and acres of white, crunchy frost. They had run down the yard and climbed onto the gate to look at all the white.

These are all the things I think of when I read this poem.
Of course, this poem is also about looking back at the city where I had felt so claustrophobic. We were just renting this house, and things hadn't quite worked out at McKellar Range, hippie central, so I wasn't exactly "home" yet, but I felt closer, and hopeful.

Birth day

This poem comes from 1978, when Margaret and I had bought the house at Horseshoe Creek. We were 17 kilometres north northeast of Kyogle, close to the creek and a bridge, in a close valley which was still largely forested. Margaret's parents came up to visit us, and Bill took lots of black and white photos of the surroundings. He developed his photos himself.

The land around the house had been kept clear of trees and in mid-summer it was rather stark. The property had been a dairy farm for maybe 70 years, from the early 1900s until the 1970s, when the Country Party told farmers to "get big or get out". Keith Thomas, from whom we bought the property, had already realised that his farm was a marginal proposition, and he closed the dairy, moved to town and just grazed some beef cattle. He hadn't lived in the house for seven years when we moved in.

Those early photos that Bill took made a good contrast to 20 years later, when all the trees I had planted had grown up, along with a lot of volunteers, like the silky oaks that sprang up everywhere once the cows were gone. The valley was reclothing itself.

At the time we arrived, a flow of people like us into the area was just beginning. Many of them were setting up in bare paddocks, just as we had at McKellar Range. Accordingly, we were the established ones, with bounty to offer. We had electricity, a phone, running water, a bath and shower, a washing machine, hot water from the slow combustion stove. People would turn up to our house to use the phone, to enjoy being in a house, and to wash clothes and clean up after heavy rain.

We all acquired a new name around this time – New Settlers. I don't know how widespread this was, for example, whether it covered the whole north coast, or extended over to Nimbin. It doesn't really matter. It certainly suited what was happening in the Kyogle area. Yes, there was fear, scorn and some animosity among locals, who wondered what we were doing in their space. But "New Settlers" summed up better what we thought we were doing than the term "hippie" which was derogatory and misleading.

Although, it is also misleading to speak as if there were some kind of cohesive movement. Everyone had their own reason for being in Kyogle, or Horseshoe Creek. Sociologically, spiritually, it was a mixed bag. A psychotherapist might have had some good theories too. But it was years later that I got clearer on the differences. In 1978 I was still focused on generating and participating in a shared ideal. I was seeing common bonds with the other new settlers and thinking that the dream was possible.

Hence, "Birth day" is a short anthem to the counter-culture ideal – that people who saw mainstream society as a mindless machine dedicated to merely material ends could show another way, a way of life based on simplicity, community and being close to the earth and its rhythms. It would be characterised by peace, love and bliss, and ahimsa (no harm).

There was a utopian aspect to this – the belief that it was possible to create a new society, to build it up practically in our physical/social environment. To live it and to show others this better life.

The obverse was the cataclysmic belief in doom, the belief that mainstream society was destroying the world. 1978 was only six years after the report of the Club of Rome, which ran computer projections saying that soon (by the 1980s and

1990s) the world would face catastrophe from multiple sources – its population was spiralling out of control, agriculture would not be able to produce enough food, pollution would poison us and natural resources would run out.

But in 1978 at Horseshoe Creek there was room for hope to be born, some signs that starting with ourselves we could show another way, and it would lead to wider change somehow. And if not, then at least we were showing what could be. Easy to say in 2007 that this was naïve, but I don't see the need to judge my position of that time harshly. Events made their own judgement on my naivety or my other faults.

There's a song that Bonnie Raitt sings, by David Gray – "Silver lining". Part of it says: "We were born with our eyes wide open, So alive with wild hoping."

That's me both then and now. The difference is that I think the dream of utopia is mistaken and misguided.

1978 was also the year that Margaret was pregnant again, and it is no coincidence that the imagery in the poem is about birth. Timothy and Andrew were born in December. A surprise. The doctor was rather casual. He had been in Kyogle for many years. He had a farm. His real interests were Percherons (draught horses), Citroens and mathematics.

I once visited him with a bad cold and sore throat. I said good morning and described my symptoms and he wrote a prescription. He nodded a couple of times (although perhaps I imagined this). After I walked out of the surgery I realised that he had completed an entire patient consultation without uttering a word. Some days he didn't talk much.

Andrew was born without any drama. He came out as babies do on good days – ruddy, animated, wet, whole. Then the doctor said, "Oh, I think there's another one there". So Timothy was born too, 20 minutes later. They were each around 2.5 kilograms, small but sound.

Forest/night/house lamps

When you drive out from Kyogle to Horseshoe Creek at night, it is quiet and dark. At least, it is servant to the moon. At intervals, you see the lights of houses, each in its own space. And the dark is not just the dark of night, it is the dark of the forest at night.

Above this is an unfathomable blue, and stars, a wide canvas for the thoughts you might project upon the sky. Sometimes the dark is in the heart also, and it seems a long way to the home that is yours.

Ming I: Darkening of the light

Ming I is Hexagram 36 in the I Ching. Its name is "Darkening of the light" (Wilhelm/Baynes edition). Over time I have found that a hexagram can keep surfacing during a particular period. This one says "The light has sunk into the earth". It refers to a situation where people of dark nature are in positions of authority and work to bring harm to the "wise and able man".

During the 1980s there were a few times when this was the case. One time was during the year after I left St Marys High School. I left there in May 1983. I had had a nice time for around five years, and I had felt supported and appreciated. But going into teaching in the first place was a corrective move only.

I had gone into a civil engineering degree from high school, a totally wrong choice. My problem was that I had no idea what to do. Father was a house painter, mother was a dressmaker. I was going to go to university, first one in the family…Mum took me to career guidance. They said I could do anything I wanted, and gave me some pamphlets, which had eight pages of text and some line drawings – doctor, lawyer, surveyor. I had no idea how those people spent their day and nothing really "grabbed" me.

In the end I made my choice on the basis of security of employment. I was good at mathematics, so a technical occupation was an open choice. And society would always need engineers. I hated it, but it took me two years to make the momentous choice to leave. Then, because I was at home with mum and I couldn't expect her to support me through three years of another university degree, I chose teaching.

With my credits from the engineering course, I could go through teachers' college in one year and get into the workforce. So I did. Then my problem was how to get to what I "really wanted to do". But the only idea in my head was writing, and I didn't want to be a journalist. So getting to "what I wanted" remained a remote dream.

Fast forward to St Marys, from December 1969 (when I left engineering) to May 1983. I had had five nice years, at a time when I needed some stability. I decided that I had to decide – either leave now or settle down and spend the rest of my working life there. It was an act of faith. I found a job in Kyogle working at a centre for unemployed youth, the Community Youth Support Scheme, at a time when the unemployment rate for youth in country areas was around 25%.

I wanted to work in the community sector. So, here goes. Leaving St Marys was hard. On my last day, there was a big gathering of pupils, not a formal occasion in the hall, but a crowd of pupils was around me after a class, and they presented me with a beautiful set of crystal glasses. Someone asked me, "Why are you leaving?" I said, "Because you can't stay at school all your life". I told them they meant a lot to me, and thanked them.

Working for a community-based committee in a small country town was a new experience. I was task-focused, and looked at the organisation in terms of its publicly-funded purpose. I was a bit slow to see that other people did not see it the same way. Some people on the committee saw it as a way of serving their own purposes, and were looking for what they could skim out of the finances. Others were on the committee for what prestige they could garner.

Some of the young people saw the centre as just a place to hang out, as long as it lasted. I wanted to turn it into a place for learning skills and for helping people to make some constructive choices about work. Some of them were friends with the chairperson of the committee who was best described as a "petty corrupt".

Things came to a head one day when the chairperson's boys decided to have a power contest with myself and Lynne (the other project officer), and take over the centre. In quick succession, both I and the other project officer had contacted the chairperson and insisted on his support, found it wanting and had resigned. The next week the federal government had dismissed the committee and suspended the project. Thence followed a six-week period of consultation by the federal department's project officers, and a public meeting to resurrect the project.

I had to choose then if I wanted to resume duties, but I decided that I had learned that lesson and didn't need to repeat it with another group of people. So I went home and tended my garden. It was 12 months before I re-entered the workforce. Other people came onto the project committee and other people came to work there, and they gave it a different focus – work and learning, so I was pleased with that. The petty corrupt people all disappeared.

In I Ching terms, I was veiling my light.

The reading

This poem (as are the next seven) is an exploration of thoughts evoked by I Ching readings. I consulted the I Ching regularly at Horseshoe Creek, both before and after Margaret left, in 1979. I was working at staying calm, peaceful, hopeful, keeping a creative direction. In the period after Margaret left I was trying to reconcile striving to remain a part of my children's lives with the need to find a new identity for myself, and one that was not bitter.

In danger

I don't remember the time this was written or the circumstances. What comes to mind? I was the general manager of the Casino Branch of the Challenge Foundation of New South Wales. Many adventures there, and traumas that are part of my life's learning. I started in February 1986. I was the first manager. Interestingly, the other candidate for the role was the petty corrupt who had been the chairperson of the Kyogle committee.

My commencement was seasoned with zest. One week after I had started work, the president of the management committee was arrested for embezzling $110,000 from the organisation. The clever thing about this was that the branch didn't have that much money. He had talked the committee into putting all its money into investments and then operating on an overdraft.

By the time his embezzlement was discovered, he had not only taken all the investments the branch had, he had left it with an overdraft of $60,000. He was arrested, charged and eventually sent to jail for six years. He had built up his position in the town through a personal style of camaraderie and charm, taking on a succession of public leadership roles. People love all that. Members of the Apex Club stood up in court and said what a great guy he was, despite the fact that he had stolen the money (and where was that money, anyway?) from people with an intellectual disability, and most of that money was from local fund-raising.

Brian was the local head of the Apex Club. And the regional director. And an alderman on the Casino Municipal Council. As well as being the local manager of a building society, where, as it happens, the Challenge Foundation had its accounts. People said that he worked hard for charitable organisations. In my conversations with him that first week on the job, he talked about the future of the organisation, what it could do and how it could grow.

I spent my second week beseeching federal and state politicians to be kind, and give us some money to keep the services going. The CEO of Challenge Foundation in Sydney came up to hold my hand, but in retrospect it occurred to me that they weren't throwing money at us. Nevertheless, the money came from the government, and we survived.

That's not why I wanted to talk about the Challenge Foundation. Once the crisis was over, I settled down to learn about disability services, to find and fulfil my mission. It was a good time to be around. The time was ripe for a change from an institutional model to services that were integrated into the community.

The model that was on offer was one that appealed to my imagination. Previously, disability services were about being a custodian of helpless people (just as Parramatta Psychiatric Centre had been). The new agenda (courtesy of Wolf Wolfensberger, for those who are familiar, and noting that Wikipedia affords him just two and half lines) was about focusing on ability rather than disability, independence rather than dependence. Teaching rather than caretaking. I was an ex-teacher. This was something I could understand, contribute to and facilitate.

What was the danger? What was the "challenge"? It was championing a shift from the dependence model to learning. Many of the staff were comfortable with dependent clients. They had a maintenance role and they could do this day after day without much involvement. Days were filled with cigarette breaks, morning and afternoon teas, contrived activities.

And then there were the parents, whose key driver was security. When I started to talk about learning and independence, they reacted with fear. Parents accused me of planning to withdraw services from their children. They were worried that, as they grew older, they would face no security of service for their children. They felt the threat of the idea that their children could be more independent than they (the parents) had been able to impart to them.

My own feeling was that the structure of the situation, and the predispositions of staff, were more responsible for the clients' lack of independence than the parents' role. There was a lot of laziness that accounted for the current reality. But I was convinced that the staff themselves would find the developmental role more rewarding than the caretaker role.

When we got underway, one of the activities that signalled the difference was the work crew that mowed lawns and did landscaping around town. Fred (now dead, lung cancer in his forties as a result of a perpetual habit of rolling his own all day), an initial sceptic, became an enthusiastic leader of a work crew. Getting something nice done in a day beat sitting around counting the hours. And his work crew were so proud – they were doing something worthwhile, which they were well capable of.

Even greater fears applied to accommodation and day services. One parent, Wilf Warren, had a son who was severely disabled, and would always be so. Wilf was old, and he needed to know that his son would be taken care of. Perhaps it is too strong to say that he hated me at the beginning, but he was a vocal opponent of any change.

I knew there were other people in my position around the same time who were ambitious, in other places. I knew they would have just said what was needed to keep things moving, to make things look like a success and "disable" any opposition. For them the immediate context was just a stepping stone to greater things. But that was not what I was about. I thought that a lot of change was possible. But I didn't think that any change was worthwhile unless the deep concerns of people like Wilf were accommodated.

All I needed was empathy. Anyone could have found themselves in Wilf's position. His son had suffered from oxygen deficiency in child-birth and had a permanent, severe intellectual disability as a result. Lifetime care. No speech, little bladder control, virtually no self-help skills. There was a moment in a meeting when I made the commitment to him publicly. I said (in appropriate language), my intent is to enhance the skills of those who are capable of being more independent, not to withdraw support from those who are not capable. We will maintain support for John, and I will fight with governments for that if I need to.

In a way, I had to beat him. But not him; rather, his fear. I was storming his fear, and to do that, I had to have the strength of dragons. And I could only do that if I was committed to bringing that same dragon horde to the doors of politicians and bureaucrats, to fight for John and his father. There was no glee in winning Wilf's support. There was passion, and compassion.

The end of this story is that, 4-5 years later, the head office of the Challenge Foundation of New South Wales indulged itself in the sordid politics of attempting to extinguish branches that did not align with its agenda of institutional preservation. It set out to destroy all the branches that were cultivating community-based services. Casino Branch was a prime candidate, and after a 12-month battle I was sacked, and they set about dismantling all the services I had created.

I had worked in Casino for over ten years by then, in three different jobs. I was probably known to 50% of the Casino population. Every one of them must have known that I was a person of integrity. But there were only a couple of people in the whole town who were prepared to stand by me. Wilf was one of them. In the universe's strange way, Wilf's son, John, died of leukaemia a couple of years later, so that Wilf did not approach his own death with the burden of worry about whether John would be provided for.

The old men have a saying

There is no need to know from whence this comes. There is in this poem the spirit of the convocation, the old men of wisdom, who watch, and at times could be said to oversee. They teach from old books. In modern days, that would be their first crime.

What is it they teach? In our age, can anyone teach? Unless they command easy listeners ("Follow my method and you will make a million dollars").

What is it they teach? Correctness, and beauty. The I Ching speaks, and the Tao Te Ching. Same source, same voice. Love the One. Live until you have made sense of this.

The dry well (Ching)

We are back at the I Ching (of course). The inexhaustible. What prompted this poem? Again, the learning that was the 1980s applies. I had no idea about popular culture during this time. I lived in silence, the garden, occasional television and no radio. The crazy hippie dreams, utopias, alternative communities, evaporated. Extremism acquired softer edges. Was it the ageing process? I decline to think so.

There is everything in the I Ching. Drought, bounty. What is hard for humans is to recognise, in the emotional or social landscape, what is one and what is the other. The outside appearance of things does not always give immediate clues. But what is one time is not the other. Sometimes the truth is that the well is dry.

So, a story about a dry well. You will have noted, that even though the well was muddy, progress followed. That is possible. The strong person wins on a wild day, branches sailing into gusts of wind with abandon, confident in strong roots in the earth. Ha! Laughing. Singing love and tenderness when all around is dryness or want.

I listen to Norah Jones. I am aware that some would find this inadequate. She is spirit of mellow, young, seemingly unschooled in bitter life. Where is the power in this? Now, suppose there comes a time when she sings her songs in acid circumstance. It would be different then. I listen in that vein, and I give an analogy.

My youngest son is now 22. He was not there when the Vietnam war waged. He was not there to be seared by Robin Williams' performance in "Good Morning Vietnam". But of all moments in that movie, none comes near to Louis Armstrong's song, "What a wonderful world". The song becomes exalted through its context. Now you see.
The I Ching? Ching means many things, for example, changes. But it also represents the well. The well is the place that anchors the town. Without the well, there is no town. In human circumstances, the lesson is to recognise when the well has dried up. For then it is time to go elsewhere.

It is not so easy for humans to recognise such things. They get attached to something, for all sorts of reasons, and do not see the clues that the attachment is no longer serving the greater purpose of their life.

Sometimes the recognition could be as simple as remembering your own commitments. When I went to Challenge Foundation in 1986, I gave myself five years. I thought that five years was an appropriate period of time in which to achieve something worthwhile and then figure out what my next project was.

And at the end of five years I had achieved a lot. I had recovered from the initial setback of the embezzlement, discovered what needed doing and what could be done, and forged ahead with new services. In the process, I learned how to be a manager – of people, money, budgets, funding, commercial projects, and new service development.

I did remember my vow at the end of five years. But there were still new projects that I thought needed my hand on the wheel, for just another 12 months or so. I wanted to "finish the job". I convinced myself that I had a duty to stay on. So what happened?

In that sixth year, the Challenge Foundation changed. Until then, Casino Branch had operated autonomously, as if there were no umbrella organisation at state level. There were 61 branches around the state, all of which operated in a similar way. We planned our own services, attracted our own funding from the federal and state governments, and managed our own finances and staff completely.

All this time there had been a petty war between the central office and the federal government about philosophy. The central office of Challenge wanted to preserve institutions, and the prevailing government philosophy was to set up community-based services and integrate people with a disability into the community as far as possible. I was part of the new wave, which was why I was successful in attracting good levels of funding for my projects.

Suddenly a new regime was in power in central office, and they had an aggressive plan. They would take power from the branches and they would thereby give themselves a solid base of power from which to force the federal government to move back to institutional services. Part of this agenda was to target the branches that were championing the new types of services and prove they were uneconomical.

They started to intrude on branch affairs and make life impossible. For example, I was told one morning to have financial statements of their specifications ready by that afternoon for tabling at a board meeting that night. I was naïve, and I thought that if I managed to jump through all the hoops they set, they would realise we were doing just fine, and leave us alone.

I hadn't met that kind of maliciousness before. The demands kept getting more and more unrealistic, and made no sense. Then I was instructed to hand over all the accounts; they would be managed from central office. I discovered that what this meant was that our bills would not be paid until they chose to pay them, and I was assailed by local businesses wanting to know when their bills would be paid.

I had an idea where this was going, but I felt I was doing the right thing, and I kept fighting. We had no debt at all, and our assets were higher than they had ever been. Our cash flow situation was tight because we had just set up a plant nursery (our first commercial venture, which was looking promising both in terms of business and as a great supported employment activity).

However, the central office had convinced the local committee that I couldn't manage things and that the branch was failing financially. I was sacked the day before Christmas, and a token administrator was sent up from Sydney to caretake branch affairs.

What he really came to do was put a price on everything so that it could be sold. What he hadn't realised was that when I had set up the plant nursery, I had built it on church land, and the arrangement with the priest was the land had to be used for disability services only. And when the priest found out that the central office was planning to sell everything, he simply put a lock on the gate. No sale.

There were fun moments in all this drama. One time, when things were intensifying, the CEO came up from Sydney – to size us up for the intended liquidation, I suppose. She asked me what accounting program we were using, and we had just implemented Mind Your Own Business. When I told her, there was an exquisite pause, and I had to explain to her that this was the name of the program. She was a rather spiteful piece of work, and this was one moment when she was set back on her heels.

She was a white South African, and she told me that community-based support services would not work. They would need so many staff that we'd have to import Asians to do the work. Just a hint of paranoia and racism there.

It was all rather ugly. After I was sacked, central office came up and told the locals that the branch was in dire straits. I knew this was a lie, and could only be the case if central office itself had extracted enough funds from the branch to put it in a deficit position. But of course I couldn't prove it at the time. Twelve months later a Board member informed me that huge "management fees" had been levied against the branch.

I spent the next 12 months trying to support two other services I had set up outside of Challenge. There was a satisfying moment at the end of that year when I found out that all the other branches of Challenge Foundation had met and had voted to disband the company. Each branch then incorporated separately. They were not going to allow the central office to do to them what it had done to Casino Branch.

Nevertheless. I had an awful lot of mud thrown at me, without any way of responding. In terms of future work, I was at a dead end. The far north coast is a small pond, and no one would employ me, even people who knew that I was competent and honest. I was a hot potato, and why put they put themselves at risk of criticism?

I went sideways by enrolling in a business degree at Southern Cross University. Over the next four years, the only work I did was casual teaching. The Education Department is a closed institution, so people there had no idea what adventures I had been having in the outside world, which did me a kindness.

I stayed in Horseshoe Creek for another 12 months after graduating, trying for jobs here, there and everywhere. I had come to terms with the fact that the well was now dry, and it was time to go overland in search of water to drink. I ended up in Sydney at the end of 1997, working as a writer and editor at CCH Australia.

The sage's undertakings

I dug through a box of my writings to see if I could find an anchor point in time for this poem. I was surprised. It was actually written during 1978, not later. When we moved to Horseshoe Creek, I was coming around to the view that a close commune was not realistic. If any form of alternative community was going to happen, it would be of a looser, more social sort, not people living with one another.

There might be cooperative activities and ventures, not intimate sharing of each other's lives. And this was how life at Horseshoe Creek evolved over the next ten years. People had their own place in the bush, and people cooperated on projects and helped each other out.

Accordingly, I gravitated to a more personal sense of awareness, experience and development, and I consulted the I Ching often. This poem was me working through the ideal of the sage, the self-mastery that was the essence of it.

Yes, indeed, an ideal, not something I could claim to be.
I also found another poem from the same period, one about Margaret and me, after five years of being together. She was pregnant with the twins at the time. The poem was of interest to me because it was written only about 12 months before she left me. I never showed it to her, it was my peace with myself:

> No, you were never one for listening,
> and I was never one for talking.
> I think you have your ideas about love

But I grew in a different way....

There's more of it. Perhaps in the next collection. In that period after she left, the words that made sense of the relationship were from Jackson Browne ("Late for the Sky") – "I don't know what you loved in me; maybe a picture of somebody you were hoping I might be".

The sage as stranger

I was moulded by Christianity while I was growing up. We attended an Anglican Church, the small weatherboard, suburban kind. But I had an intelligent bunch of peers, including rational Harold, who was just a few years older than me and who for a time went to Moore Theological College.

Harold helped us all to think about things, and not accept what was said in church or written in the Bible at face value. He called us out of that hypnotised state where ritualised words substitute for facing the risk of finding your own understanding.

So. The concept that kept coming to me was this idea of Jesus as the stranger, the one who came out of nowhere and who did not have the stamp of approval of the official church people of the day. The one who says, "Listen to this. What do you think? Watch what I do. What do you think?"

In the I Ching, the sage too is a stranger. He (or she) knows himself as spirit and experiences life that way. He brings that essence (love, truth) into each moment and situation. He embodies paradoxes – obedience, power.

This model I emulated but poorly, but it has been a touchstone over the years when situations have seemed to be spinning out of control or have become oppressive. I come back to it, I remember not to fall into the illusion of doom.

The sage as stranger also guided me in work. I am 57 now and I've never had a cohesive, goal-driven career plan. Part of me envies those people who never had to make a choice. Like Tom Young at Horseshoe Creek, who left school and became a cabinet-maker, and gradually evolved into a unique craftsman, a maker of high-class period reproduction furniture.

I met Tom just after Margaret and I bought the house at Horseshoe Creek. He and Nancy had bought land near us, jointly with Phillip and Dale. The four of them were building a huge, double house in mud brick – the mud brick mansion as it became known. I used to spend days with them helping to make mud bricks and offer my unskilled labour.

Tom always had work making furniture, and he was always extending himself, learning something new. Always becoming better. He was the quintessential expert, with a deep understanding and love of his craft. And he worked right up until his death, as everyone knew that he would. There were no doubts here about what he was on earth to do. The Old Testament phrase "the salt of the earth" is about Tom.

Against this, I was a boat adrift in a bay. I had gifts and hankerings, no clear shape or direction, and no models to follow. By the late seventies I had already spent ten years in teaching and it was merely a default choice. But if I look back now at the period when this poem was written, I did make some progress, and the I Ching was part of that.

I thought, if I am not a "salt of the earth" person, then I am a stranger, and I wait upon moments, I look for what needs to be done. After I left St Marys High School and took up my first job in the community sector, I thought of myself as an "odd job" man. I thought working with unemployed youth in Kyogle was something that needed doing, and I could contribute something worthwhile.

And I took up coordinating adult education in Kyogle, which had just commenced in a modest way. I built up a regular program of courses over the next three years and saw good things happen there. It was the first forum where "locals" and "new settlers" could come together during this transitional time, when new settlers were still arriving and some locals were reacting with resentment and hostility. I remember courses in bonsai, massage and short story writing where there were people from both camps, each realising the other was human.

K'un (Receptive)

This I Ching hexagram is 2, K'un, The Receptive. There are six lines in a hexagram, each of which can be unbroken (yang, male, active) or female (yin, female, receptive). K'un is made of six yin lines, thus it takes the image, The Receptive. One rendition of this hexagram (Wu Wei, 2005, p 81) says "sublime success will come to you if you are willing to follow good advice, are open to new information, yield to others' ideas and wishes, follow wise leaders who have worthy goals, work hard, cooperate, and avoid taking on leadership".

In the Wilhelm/Baynes edition, which was the one I had in the 1970s, it illustrates the qualities of K'un with the image of the mare. The mare combines the strength and swiftness of the horse with the gentleness and devotion of the cow. The essential quality it advises is to act "in conformity with the situation", to learn what is demanded of you and to follow accordingly.

This hexagram also says there are times when we need to be alone. There is a sacred hour when one must do without companions in order to clarify what one must do. The image of K'un (the doubling of the receptive trigrams) includes the idea of the earth that carries all things that live and move upon it. Per Wilhelm/Baynes: "The earth in its devotion carries all things, good and evil without exception".

There was an obscure movie in the 1970s, *High Road to China*, which contains the line "The ox is slow, but the earth is patient". The idea that emerges through this hexagram is that we are but players in an ages-long drama. We may do our part, but we will not preside over the defeat of all evil. In fact, in order to do our part in the ages-long drama, we must be the earth, not the judge. We must support all people and all things without discrimination.

It was good that I had this guidance at the beginning of the 1980s. I needed it to guide me through the dramas of separation and divorce, community endeavours and the Challenge Foundation. And when I come back to the opening comments for this hexagram, the first words are: "sublime success". I see that there are different kinds of success.

There is success that is material – victories, rewards, money and recognition. "Sublime success" is qualitatively different to this. It is exalted success, it is success that moves you across a threshold, it is success that evokes wonder. It is soul-deep. Sublime success delivers you to yourself, your "real" self.

I think that I found it difficult to see this at many points during the 1980s. I was more conscious of defeat and failure. A failed marriage, another catastrophic relationship, children living at a distance, a disastrous ending at the Challenge Foundation.

However, even when I felt I was at the bottom of a pit, and people in Casino and at Challenge had treated me badly, the thought that often filtered through the depression was, "Okay, suppose you are right – it all ended disastrously. Did you do what you thought was right? Are you ashamed of yourself? Would you rather be some of those people who fought you, the ones that were dishonest, deceitful and callous?

I had to concede that I preferred to be me, even with the defeats and failures. Perhaps it takes a long time to see, but I understand now, that was sublime success – when you know that in practical terms, you could have done better, you could have been smarter and might have been able to carve out a worldly victory, but essentially, you are not sorry you took the stand you did. You stood for what was good, what was right.

I have been faced with situations recently that bore an uncanny parallel to some of the situations I faced in the 1980s. And my first reactions were not a lot different. I was angry, offended at behaviour that was dishonest, manipulative, corrupt. And then I was emotionally pulled by the idea that "it was all happening again". Cosmically, did this mean that I had learned nothing in the 1980s? Was I doomed to repeat unsavoury episodes?

There were amusing distinctions. I was on the other side of the fence. I was the president; he was the employee. I was constrained not to treat this situation as an opportunity for revenge for the past (despite Rohan's advice to bring out the sword and chop him into small pieces). The big obstacle was thinking the situation was out of the control of the universe and its wisdom. What is immediately in front of you can loom large.

But then, what do the old men teach from their books? Correctness, and beauty. So I took it step by step. I had meetings, I gave instructions, I gave latitude and opportunities. And I kept track. What I found was lies, bluff, failure to fulfil, scorn, attempted haughtiness. After I'd had enough, I went digging into his past. I had a list of issues about his performance as long as my arm.

But I remembered that people like this have displayed their penchant before. So I went digging further into his past. I had done this before, when I had been burned by a person I had appointed as a manager, during the Challenge years.

As it turned out, the answer was simple. One of the referees he had used was a fabrication. The person was real, but he had not been a previous manager. He was a friend who was willing to prostitute himself. So I was able to persuade my board to dismiss him, without the extended fuss of "investigating his performance" and making "judgements" about his ability to do the job.

Simple. Conman. Incompetent at the job, and hoping to make his way with froth and bullying. As if it would work in the long run anyway. And for me? A prompt solution, and very little stress. Maybe some wisdom after all. Maybe even some managerial competence. Afterwards, more confidence. Validation of a sort. K'un is the unbound, a dancer in the joy of the lord.

The last song

Date? February 1972. A long way back. Before the accident. Before Margaret. I played the guitar then. I wrote songs. I was teaching. I was at the House of the New World, with a New Age Jesus and cultural revolution in my head. I was at Sydney University, studying for a BA – philosophy and education, of sorts.

Just me aware of my proclivities, the dangers of the self. My heart cast to the realm, out of necessity if not predilection. Sing for other ears than your own.

The last supper

My goodness. Some of my poems scare me. Where do they come from? I give you a specific date, and there is even a diary for this period of time. 24 December 1973. The day before Christmas. Special. Why?

My motor bike accident had been in January of that year. I had been in bed or in plaster for most of the year. By November I was walking again. I had a walking stick for a while.

My big sister, Helen, was getting married. In Hobart, Tasmania. So I decided I would fly down (I confess, this was my first plane trip), go to the wedding and then hitchhike around Tasmania. Hitchhiking was not taboo then. It was a bit maverick, but not tainted with the spectre of murderers.

I went to the wedding. White, church, ceremony, all that. Bride, groom. And afterwards, go. I had upset Margaret. We were "together". She had expected to come too. But I needed to do something alone after months of hospital. The biggest challenge of being hurt and helpless was the loss of independence.

During the weeks of skin grafts, I had the use of one hand. I couldn't cut up my meals myself. The nurses used to do that for me. But it was a big hospital, and often there was no one available to cut up my food. The nurses were busy. So I had a choice. I could eat my food like an animal, or wait. I waited. My food went cold. Many nights. The nurse would turn up after 30 minutes and cut it up. I would eat cold food.

So Margaret didn't understand why I wanted to do Tasmania alone, independent. I was emotionally raw. I was filled with a multitude of emotions. Freedom, gratitude. I had my leg. I could walk again.

For this poem I was sitting in the botanical gardens in Hobart one afternoon. There was a greenhouse in the gardens that had the encrustations of time and contentment, a bond with the earth that made it easy for fairies to exist. It was cloudy and cool and the fairies may have been peeping out from behind pots and ferns. Totally at ease in their surroundings.

I kept a diary of my travels around Tasmania. It was a surreal experience. I met many people, who represented so much of what was happening in the world at that time, the currents, the quest for emergence beyond the heaviness of established patterns of life. Another time I will share that.

I believe that Jesus loves this poem.

I would like to end it here, but I realise that there are those who did not have my benign upbringing in Sunday School. I refer you to the New Testament book of Luke, Chapter 19. Perhaps I relate to this story because Zacchaeus was short.

The setting is Jericho. Jesus was passing through, and was at this time very popular with the crowds. His message was abroad – live with a clear heart and gratitude. A new day, the kingdom of God. We know this from what Zacchaeus said: Look, sir, I am going to give half my property to the poor, and if I have cheated anybody I will pay him back four times the amount.

The Sunday School song is this:
>Zacchaeus was a little man
>And a very little man was he,
>He climbed into a sycamore tree
>For he wanted the Lord to see.
>And when the Lord came passing by
>He looked into the tree
>And he said, Zacchaeus you come down
>For I'm going to your house for tea.

(I can sing that for you if you want. One doesn't forget.)

The poem is about the reaction that people had to this incident, including the disciples. In verse 7 we read: They (the crowd) all complained when they saw what was happening. "He has gone to stay at a sinner's house". (And Jesus would shake his head.)

Being in the gardens at the time, I was inspired to include a thought from elsewhere in the gospels. Earlier in Luke (Chapter 12), there is the classic piece about the flowers (in the Jerusalem Bible it is headed: "Trust in Providence"):
"Think of the flowers; they never have to spin or weave; yet, I assure you, not even Solomon in all his regalia was arrayed like one of these. Now if that is how God clothes the grass in the fields which is there today and thrown into the furnace tomorrow, how much more will he look after you, you men of little faith!"

(Your Father knows that you need things to eat and things to drink, but set your heart on his kingdom, and these other things will be given to you as well.) (And yes, for the pedantic, the rendition is from the Jerusalem Bible, 1966.)

Onward. Living in the extravagance of universal love. Harvest the truth from wherever it grows.

The end

The quote at the beginning of this book talked about staying in the wilderness for too long. Yet there is also the truth that at times we must go alone into the wilderness "where the angels will minister to us". There is the time of love and there is a time for armour. Teasingly, the French word for love is *amore*. The distance between love and armour, and vice versa, is not far – a reminder for those who tend to become set in their ways.

And I say:
"I have evidence. The universe is kind."

The author

Born in Sydney in 1950. Grew up in Greenacre. Was schooled and churched in the usual ways. Went to University of New South Wales and didn't complete engineering. Went to University of Sydney and didn't complete Arts. Became a high school teacher of mathematics. After three years, left and became psychiatric nurse. Went to Mackay, Queensland and taught mathematics there.

Moved to far north coast of New South Wales in 1976 and ended up in Kyogle. Stayed for 20 years. In that time, three partners, five children, several gardens.

Numerous jobs – teacher (manual arts and maths) at St Marys, Casino; project officer, program for unemployed youth in Kyogle; project officer (community services) for Casino Municipal Council; adult education coordinator in Kyogle; manager for Challenge Foundation (disability services).

Wrote *Places in the Bush* (a history of Kyogle Shire) in 1988 and *Kyogle Public School Centenary Book* (1995).

Went back to university – Southern Cross University at Lismore. Finished this time – Bachelor of Business (Honours, University Medal).

Ended up back in Sydney as a writer and editor for CCH Australia – business information services (human resources, employment law, training and development).

Went back to university (definitely a recidivist) and obtained Master of Education (Online Education) from University of Southern Queensland.

Became single again.

Wrote book on ethics – *Human values and ethics in the workplace* – in 2006. It becomes (in 2007) a self-published shelf companion to this book and *Flames in the open*, my other book of poems and stories.

Working from home now, mostly; writing, mostly.

Mission: To see truth and say what is helpful.